BENA

Ugochukwu Durueke

BENA
Ugochukwu Durueke

"Poetry is an echo, asking

a shadow to dance."
- Carl Sandburg

Copyright © 2023 by Ugochukwu Wilson Durueke

No part of this publication may be reproduced, distributed or transmitted in any form or by any means, including recording, photocopying, or any other methods without the prior permission of the publisher.

In order to obtain permission to use material from this book, please make a written request to
udurueke@yahoo.com.

For my daughter, Praise.

Acknowledgement

The production of this work of art would not have been possible without the assistance of God, my family and Miss Mavalyn Cole. I am thankful. My gratitude also goes to my supporters who not only purchased my books in the past but who celebrate me whenever I reach a milestone in literature.

Preface

'BENA' is my third collection of poems. The poems speak to personal, national and international situations and issues. The poems are laden and heavy with powerful emotion.

I am sure readers will not only relate to life's issues and conditions explored therein but will enjoy the poems.

Happy reading!

WHERE IS LOVE?

The world is a place
Where people hurt
One another physically
Emotionally and verbally
Sometimes we call
Such acts abuse and crime
We live in a world
In which racism
Prejudice and discrimination
Hate and segregation
Stereotyping and xenophobia
Hold sway
From the United States of America
To Australia
From Norway to South Africa
From islands to main lands
Ironically, we sing
We talk about love
But, do we truly know love
When we refuse to help
The less-fortunate
And the less privileged?
Do we have love
When we insult
Ridicule and belittle others?
Have we love
When we hate people

'Cause of their religious beliefs
Political persuasions
Their nationalities
'Cause of their economic backgrounds
Social standings
Do we have love in our hearts
When we despise others
'Cause of their looks
And their accent?
Where was love
During the Holocaust
Where was love
During first and second World Wars
Where was love
During the Rwanda and Burundi genocide
Where was love
In the days of Apartheid in South Africa
Where is our love
In all terrorist attacks
Where is love
In the mass deportation
Of people of Haitian origin
By the authorities
In the Dominican Republic
Love, love where are you?

FACEBOOK

You're the web
That links humans
Across the globe
Social boundaries
Cultures and geographical zones

You're the creator
Of avenues for relationships
As you make people
Meet first time
And several times

You're the finder
Of long 'lost' friends
And acquaintances
Putting smiles on faces
And joy in hearts

You're a great reservoir
Of data
Always dipping your hand
In the well of memories
To remind people of others' birthdays

THE RESOLUTE

I dislodged a hive of wasps
For a moment,
They were in disarray
Shortly, they regrouped
Ready to rebuild
I was in awe
Because of their resilience
None bemoaned their misfortune
And dislodgement
Instead, all hands
Went to work
Regardless of what life
Had thrown at them
On reflection,
I wondered what life
Would be like
If people learnt a lesson
From wasps.

THE DROUGHT

The clouds rested
Heavily upon the village
Making people scurry out
To take in their items
For they thought the rains imminent
After awhile,
The sun came out
And gradually dispersed
The pregnant clouds
And took her majestic place
Poised to place
The sons of men
Under sweltering heat,
Again, she had dashed
The hope of the parched
And thirsty earth

THE WHIFF

The whiff struck my attention
I lost myself in the woods
Of meditation
In the wilderness of philosophy
I pondered the brevity
Not just the puff
But the human and her mortal neighbours
Shortly, I returned to the physical
Yet, I wondered if all that had gone
The way of mortals
Would ever return some day
To embrace the din, the drudgery
The dream and the aspirations
The pain, the joy and the pace
Of this life.

THE CHAMPIONSHIP

It's time
For sprint championship
The clash of the athletes
The stadium is packed
And abuzz with life
It's time
For the clash of nerves
Athletic skill
Matching athletic prowess
It's time
For cheering
And jeering
It's time
For the joy of winning
And the pain of losing
But, for me,
It's time
For togetherness

DILEMMA

I see this isle
A piece of natural beauty
A part of me tells me
To preserve this setting
Keep it pristine and unspoilt
To respect and not tilt
The ecological scale and balance
Even in the face of growing unemployment
Joblessness and underdevelopment
But then, another part of me
Keeps egging me on
Telling me to give this piece of nature
To foreigners
For technological development
And its attendant employment prospects
So in this context
I ask myself: what must I do?
But, I hear the voices
Of my creditors reminding me of the loans
And my financial obligations
I shudder and wish
I never had any dealings
With lending agencies
But, I'm Jamaica
I must rise amidst challenges
And fight for my survival

(The plan to offer Goat Island to the Chinese for Logistic hub, in Jamaica.)

TWO MOUTHED

As I grow older
I learn deeper
Lessons about humanity
About mankind
People come to you
And laugh with you
But, behind your back
They laugh at you
They pretend to support
You and your interest
And venture
But, in their hearts
And in your absence
They fight you
Put stumbling blocks
In the way of your progress
Should misfortune
Intrude in your life
They express 'sympathy'
And claim 'empathy'
But in their minds
They gloat over your mishap
What a two-faced humanity!

ODE TO CUCUMBER

This green coat of life
Sometimes smooth
Sometimes rough and bumpy
The covering of white
Water exuding body
A case of rich nutrients
This biochemical element
Facilitator of life
Cut in slices
Maybe not
Sunk into and chewed
Mouth-watering
Yet, with indescribable taste
Here is my ode to this richness
Refreshment and health-giving
Tube of greenery

BRING BACK MY SISTERS

Where were you
When the hoodlums
Came and herded my sisters
Out of the citadel
Of learning

Where were you
When the hooligans
Drove off with my sisters
And shot at those
Who darted off for safety

Where were you
When Boko Haram
Struck, causing pain,
Grief
And despair
In the heart of civilised people?

I know you were drunk
With the fat from national oil
Intoxicated by the tonic
Of ill-gotten gains
Stupefied by political wine

Arise now, arise now
From your stupor

For kindred spirits
All over the world
Are calling for my sisters

I need them back
I need my sisters
Whatever it takes
I need them back
I need them back!

THE FAMILY HISTORY

Under the mango tree
Grandpa told me
Stories of my family's past
At long last

He told me
Stories of my great people
Of my heritage not so little
A people who are free

He delved into memory
And ancient history
Of a family
With great ancestry

From there
I learnt of Durueke, my forebear
Of Isiguzo, my great-grandpa, the legend
To the end

I still remember the incident
Which within me
Has become an event
In which I learnt much about me

USAIN BOLT, My Teacher

Injury afflicted you
Kept you away
From the tracks
From your familiar
And cherished territory
For sometime
But, you rose above it all

The game began
Expectations went high
Nerves stretched
Along the way you stumbled
But your resilience prevailed
With the strength of a lion
You powered yourself on to semi-final

Time for the final came that Sunday
The world stood still
This human cheetah sped on
Fought and shrugged off
His greatest opponent
Powered on to victory and glory
Shaming the naysayers

Usain Bolt, you're my teacher
You're my hero
Like you. I'll never allow

Adversities and challenges
To weigh or pin me down
For I can rise
And grab victory!

IAAF Championship Beijing 2015

THE TREE

<u>Before</u>
Tall and towering
Full of greenery
Plenitude of leaves
Branches stretching out
Canopying large space
Fat, unembraceable trunk
With a network of wiry,
Stringy parasitic flora
Huge roots that burst
The earth, the asphalted way
Even breaking a fence
This gigantic wind-breaker
A shelter from the sun
A habitat for birds

<u>Now</u>
Full of brown leaves
Gradually dying branches
The result of some chemical
Injected in this huge body
Of foliage
Whitening, drying up
A picture of death
A slowly dying
Botanical giant

GOOD-LOOKING DEATH MACHINE

Broad dark spectacles
Neck bedecked with gold chains
Body hugging white suit
Complemented with
A pair of white
Gorgio Fellantini shoes
Brief case clutched
By his right hand
The left showcasing
A big Rolex watch
His smile reveals
Two gold teeth
Which festoon his dentition
This is the vanity guy
Waiting for another teenage girl
To trap with his wiles
And guiles
Waiting to welcome
Another unsuspecting
And naïve young female
To his web of deceit
This vanity guy is death's machine
Awaiting another female
To receive his life-ending discharge

FOR MY GRANDMA, ROSALINE ANUKWA

My grandmother Rosaline
A great woman
Quite trim, slim and fit
An epitome of black beauty
Physically strong
And graceful in her movement
I remember the past
When I was in my maternal home
She doted on me and my siblings

Grandma Rosaline
Was a woman of principle
A great disciplinarian
Childish misdemeanour
Drew her stern look
A serious look which spoke volumes
And put children back
On good behavioural track
Back to decency and decorum

Grandma Rosaline
Emotionally strong and elastic
Endured agonies and pain
Which could have destroyed man
The deaths of her beloved husband
Papa Barthelome

Her first son, Lawrence
Her daughter, Eunice (my forever loved mother)
Shook the bars of grandma's heart

My grandma Rosaline
Lived and fought the adversities of life
Overcame the challenges
And the rigors of human existence
With immeasurably great vigor
She wrestled with negative situations
In a painful and rough
Journey of 106 years
I thank God for her.

Rest well colossus!

TRUE RELIGION

Some people hold
On to the divine
Pledge their souls' allegiance
To Him, enslave self
To do's and don't's of their faith
Choosy beings they become
Of foods, beverages, clothes
And lifestyle
But, they hate their fellow humans
Imprison others in the dungeons
Of their hard hearts
I wonder: what kind of god
Such profess and worship?
True religion awaits people
Calling them and crying out,
'It's in your soul
To love others
So as to please the spirit
True religion is not talk
But deed that mirror
The character of the Divine One

THE DISABLE

I live in a harsh world
Full of ruthlessness
With a child
A victim of disability
Some say he's useless
And a great challenge
Throw him out
For a peace of mind
For good mental health
To pursue greater economic interest
But, I pay no heed
For my heart is saturated
With great fatherly love
Yes, I struggle daily
With my child's condition
I struggle with the challenges
Birthed by his incapacity
Yet, I persevere
And hold my cross
I close my eyes
Picture him out of the fold
I shudder, I tremble and wonder
Would I be able
To face the guilt factor?
To the world out there
It seems a solution
So easy, so cool

But will I be able
To deal with it
At the table and bedtime?

THE FURIOUS METAL

The black and white television
Was on, showing us
A football match
Shortly, the reception
Became poor, ricy and 'grainy'
The living room turned
Into a sick place
Of sighs, fuss and vexation
My young brother
Sprang out of the room
For the antenna
The antenna had beads
Of raindrops from the afternoon drizzle
As he tried to turn
The antenna for better reception
The current charged element
Flung him up
The force of gravity
Took him down
My paternal grandma
Seeing his state
Rushed to save him
But, the furious metal
Flung the two of them up
From the high
Down they came
Grandma let out

A cry of pain!

SCHAEFER'S HOUSE

Schaefer was a brown
Sixty-five year old woman
Who adored her house
And cherished her environment
She would come out
In the mornings
And cherished her environment
She would come out
In the mornings
And scope the milieu
If displeased, she would
Eject Mr. Bell, a seventy year old
Who ran errands for her
She was so particular
About her house
That she never allowed
Many people from the community
To enter her premises
After some moons
She took ill
Battled with the condition
And went the way of mortals
A few days after Schaefer's funeral, some people moved
Into the house
And turned it into a free for all place
Death is indeed

A powerful phenomenon
As its pangs
Bind the high and mighty
Were Schaefer to see
What's become of her house
She would have a stroke,
Perhaps a heart attack!

THE MIGRANT

Vera wanted to go overseas
Made several attempts
To get a VISA
But failed
She complained bitterly
In the shop
Where she was working
Years later,
Her daughter filed for her
The process ran its course
And bore fruit
Vera took a flight
To Delaware
A place where
She felt so lonely
She almost became mentally deranged
After two years
She flew back
To her island home
In the West Indies
Vera vowed to not go
Back to the United States
Friends and relatives
Begged her to return
To the United States
So that her Permanent Residency Status
Would not be revoked

But she refused
In her cognitive world
'The United States is good
For the young not the aged'
Vera's daughter called
Day and night
Threatening
Pleading
And coaxing
With face awash with tears
Vera painfully returned
To the United States

MY VIEW OF POETRY

My poetry
Is in the open
Requires no microscope
Needs no telescope
To scope it
It's crystal clear
Reading my works
Is not like trying
To see through an opaque glass
For I believe
That poetry should be
Man's friend and companion
Not an alien being to him/her
Poetry should not
Give one a headache
But have interesting
Conversations with one
For I believe
That the beauty of the art
Should not be coated
And concealed
But should sparkle
Like a mirror in the sun
For I believe
That poetry should not
Be some mythical unreachable water
To thirsty and dehydrating humankind

But an ever present fountain
From which springs
Some refreshing water
I believe
That poetry should be
Healthy for the head
And heart of man.

THE REPORTER

He had been feeding
the landlord with news
of the tenant
Every week he made overseas calls
to report him the 'the whiteman',
the inheritor of the house
the reporter living nearby
in a makeshift dwelling
tad an agenda to cross
the lines of social hierarchy
Some moons later,
the landlord came
Day after day he went out
with the news carrier
to shop, to drink
and to dine in a restaurant
They spiralled with this cycle
of activities daily
The 'whiteman' gave
the tenant eviction notice
before going back to his abode
overseas
Smilingly, this news carrier,
this scheming reporter,
moved in, and planted flowers
He would come out
and saunter around the house

a picture of self-satisfaction

THE VOW

They took the vow
before the servant of God
to hold and to have
till death do they part
Life rolled on with jollity
for them
years passed sickness
Struck him
It's a kidney disease
She began to drift
away from him
The vow made
no sense to her
For she believed in
'for better' not 'for worse'
'in health' not in sickness
She found another man
A paramour
Who gave her a baby
The 'sanctioned one'
suffered ill-health
till he died
she had no shame
No conscience
this is the way of the world.

THE WOMAN AND THE DOG

She left the front door open
went to the kitchen
suddenly her eyes caught
a shadow of a being
that had just darted across
she wasn't sure what it was
momentarily she got confused
inactivity held her back
but shortly, an unbearable
stench pervaded the place
this jolted her into moving
a quest for the cause
the sight of a dirty, smelly
and sore-filled dog greeted her
the dog ran back in one room
as she impulsively sped off
to call for help

WHAT A BLOW!

The mother left him
with his father
A few months later
she died
The father bonded
with him and grew him
for sometime
Their lives expressed
great filial affinity
When the son turned twelve
terminal sickness grabbed
the father
Its stranglehold weakened him
The boy ran errands for him
till he dwindled
and died
Now, no mother
No father
Peers became his parents
his guardians and advisers
Though uncles still around
he stopped attending school
Metamorphosed into a man of the street
an idler and marijuana smoker
What a blow nature
and society had dealt
a young man !

THE CUT

She had borrowed a lump some
to revamp her flagging business
Business began to boom
Milk and honey began to flow
One afternoon,
a gunman held her up at the stall
before everyone's view
She told him
that she had a loan to repay
but he pointed a gun at her
fear of losing her money
consumed her ____ not worried
about dying
She bent down
pretending to take up
the money-bag
In a flash reached
her razor-sharp machete
and cut the gunman's left hand off
The dismembered element
jerked and jerked
With fright and sharp pain
he bolted away
with a trail of blood
Shortly, people swarmed
the scene
She licked her lip

with her tongue
Her heart must have said
'Serves him right.'

A MALE'S LIFE

The life of a true male
is full of thistle and thorns
Ti's a rugged terrain
From childhood
he is schooled
to be tough
and to be rough
He is told
regardless of bad circumstances
not to cry
but to try
to bottle up his feelings
of pain
of hurt
of frustration
When he becomes a full man
he has to work hard
to provide for self and family
He has to fight life
fight for life
and fight for his wife

ELEMENTARY SCHOOL DAYS

In a village primary school
my classmates and I
came out at recess
Didn't have money
to buy lunch
so we decided
to leave our mouths open
so that the sweet smell
of freshly baked bread
from a bakery nearby
could waft into our being
and full us up
Years later,
as an adult, I reflect on
the folly and innocence
of childhood
With hungry stomach
we had to learn
our Arithmetics, English
and General Science
To and from school
I walked long distances
on many a sunny
and rainy day
The life lesson learnt
in my childhood days
prepared me for the painful

and agonizing experiences
of adult life

THE DEAD BABIES SCANDAL

Some fruits of the womb
Considered unripe were
in their incubation world
Innocent souls they were
One day,
the destroyer came,
a vicious element
dealt them deadly blows – unseen
while medics were wide awake
and looking on
The life journey of the babies
was cut short
Now,
the deaths caused a political storm
while the bereaved families
sob, grieve and mourn
Each time the issue
surfaces in the media
tears course down some cheeks
the depth of the pain
in the bereaved hearts
gets deeper

- Death of 19 premature babies in a hospital in Kingston, Jamaica 2015

AT HOME WITH MYSELF

The circumstances of my birth
have no bearing on my future
for I have to rise
and chat the course of my life

Where my life began
isn't an issue to me
for I have to rise
to climb the mountains of life

The colour of my skin
matters not to me but my character
and contributions to human
development count

I'm proud of my background and identity
I refuse to be defined and characterised
by prejudiced, racial comment made about
me
I'm truly home with myself!

THE TOXIC 'LEADER'

I know a leader
a self – absorbed leader
who thinks that he
knows everything and
others know nothing
So whatever he says
becomes a law
This 'leader' has no respect
no regard for others
and their views – a psychopathic destroyer
of emotion
He brags so much about
his 'achievements', 'accolades'
and qualifications
This 'leader' feels and behaves
as if he is the best thing
the earth could offer
His narcissistic and 'egomaniacal'
tendencies will be his undoing
and downfall.

THE BARBER BOY

He took up some piece
of a broken bottle
since he had no shaver
or razor
he scraped the sides
of his head with the
sharp piece giving
himself some 'vulture – head
-like' hairstyle
As he walked into the classroom
the place went ablaze
with laughter, snickering,
ridicule and thunderous voices
This is a barber poster boy
He is now the centre of attraction
A new celebrity
He is enjoying his new status
with his 'John Crow' hairstyle
But, to the intelligent ones in class
his scraped hair had given him
the reputation of a mad man

John Crow is a Jamaican term for 'vulture'

DOMEKE'S RUN

The men came on the compound
that night and tried
to capture him so he could
be earmarked and dedicated
to the local deity and his lineage subjected
to ostracism by pedigreed
families, the free-born and titled
men and women. But Domeke shuddered
at the thought of being branded
an '*osu*'. So having sensed
the arrival of the invaders, he scaled
the fence, dissolved
in the darkness and blended
with the forest that bordered
his home. He groped
and was tripped
by a yam mound
He rose and moved
On elements of woodland he stepped
In his mind he heard
his late mother's call and he turned
to the way that led
to Umunkwodu, and journeyed
He struggled and struggled
until he emerged
at the hamlet, his mother's kindred
received him and sheltered

him. Years passed
Domeke returned
to raise a large family and brood
His generations are thankful that he fled
from that which would've trapped
them into being less-privileged.

JIMBA

His name was Jimba
A thin, wiry man
who walked slowly with foot
slightly bent
He had 'an answer'
to every problem in the village
Some saw him as a liar
others who were gullible
got taken in by his deceitfulness
At my father's invitation. He would
come to my home to give my siblings
and me a hair cut
He would apply some slimy liquid
on our foreheads and use his
blades to shape our hairlines
The sliminess usually sent chills
down my spine
Upon completion of this job
my father would give
a few kobo*, and off he went

*Kobo is a Nigerian coin.

OLU UBI

Farm work would see us
rise early in the mornings
walk great distances
in a world of flora
sometimes totally enveloped
in a universe of greenery
we would cut, chop and pluck
thistle, thorns and grass
we would gather the uprooted elements
and set them ablaze until
they formed ichekiri oku*
which later decorated
our faces with black marks
making us look like
some masquerades as we moved
the burnt out elements
from one part of the farm
to next
Later, we planted crops
from dawn to dusk
After the season of cultivation
we would tend our plants
by weeding the farm lands
Our care for the botanical beings
continued until harvest.

AEDES EGYPT MOSQUITO

You are much talked about
Dreaded alot
A carrier of ailment
which doles out
undesirable and unwanted element

You give out
dengue virus
chikungunya virus
zika virus
This is your lot

Your handiwork keeps scientists working
wondering and investigating
testing and re-testing
checking and re-checking
trying and re-trying

Your work makes humans
restless, edgy, listless
and full of pain and aches
It eats the financial resources
of responsible and responsive governments

A GREAT CHANGE

The people had created a clime
of horrible slime
and unbearable grime
which couldn't be changed with dime
but, one day Mister Rhyme
felt it was time
to use soap and lime
to clean the unsightly clime
and to chime
in a place in its prime

SAVED BY DEATH

The ruthless dictator
with the instrumentality
of state power and 'the law'
slammed his opponents
and dissidents in maximum
security prison
waiting for his appointed time
to take them to the slaughter house

But the One who controls
time and tide
The Supreme One
allowed coronary problem
to send him to a place of no return
His second - in – command
said to the inmates,
"Go, for death has released you."

Kirikiri Prison * spewed out
What it had

Kirikiri is a maximum security prison in Nigeria.

LAST FIGHT IN HIGH SCHOOL

He was nicknamed 'Aristotle'
a chemistry brain he was
one day at his commerce class
he 'engineered' his teacher
to punish me unjustly
What happened?
I was in my seat
when the commerce teacher
walked in
'Aristotle' told the teacher
to send me out of the class
'cause I wasn't one of her students
he lied I was I was I his seat
The teacher asked me to step out
and kneel down in the sun
This I did until the end
of the class an hour later
When the teacher left at the end
of her class, I went to 'Aristotle'
to warn him against playing
such pranks next time
but he laughed and laughed
and 'led' me on to a dead – end
where he suddenly turned
and head – butted me
I tasted my blood and the world
of injustice I had just suffered

flashed on my mind
my adrenaline gave me
a bitter taste in my mouth
I lunged at 'Aristotle', lifted
him with all my might, slammed
him on the dry, dusty and thirsty
ground, a huge cloud of
dust almost engulfed us
I pummelled him
scooped some sand
from the earth and dumped
such all over his face
some got in his eyes, nostril and mouth
'Aristotle' struggled to rise
but I pinned him down
I punched his face harder
even as it was bloodied
he began to shake with rage
I knew that once he was up
the real fight would ensue
'Aristotle' eventually sprang up
but I kept raining punches
on him
he threw a few punches
which never caught me
he was no match for a man
with venomous anger like me
Some students rushed us
and Two teachers came

and stopped the fight
'Aristotle' was costumed
with dirt

IBO

Many moons ago
Battered, bruised and dehumanised
Psyche badly hurt
Suffered aches and pain
But, Ibo remained undaunted
And undefeated
Now,
She is rising
The challenges
And machinations
Of enemies notwithstanding,
Ibo's rising and rising!

THE NEW TEACHER

She came into the school
exuding confidence
ready to impart knowledge
to the future of the society
shortly, the joy turns
into discouragement, dismay
and displeasure
for the future of the nation
does not want what
she has to offer from
her intellectual reservoir

PITY FOR THE HIGH

You advised them
to scrape the dry pot
of their drained finances
to pay for the test
Plan was for you
to prepare and groom them
with your bountiful intellectual resources
Having made the sacrifice
of paying for the test with
their widow's mite
you turned your back on them
Now, the test starts
and you ask me:
where are they?
Are they in the exam room?
Let's hope they're there
I'm shaken by your ambivalence
by your lack of empathy
towards the poor
I turn aside and cry
for what the mighty
have made of the ordinary
in our society
always working hard
to keep them poor, common
and unaccomplished
It's a pity for the high

in the society

THE DEATH OF TWO MISSIONARIES

The two men came
worked tirelessly for several years
touching lives positively
providing material help
spiritual guide to the needy
foreigners to this land
they were
But, some men
evil men killed the two men
two men who had
given sacrificially
for the well-being of natures
What man has made of life!

THE ADVISER

Crises came into their relationship
gossip, insinuations and contentions
raged and raged
you slipped into the situation
and stoked the fire
fanned the amber
of disunity and disharmony
you, who never used to say,
'Hello' to them before, now
have become the self-appointed
adviser to one party
doling out poisonous advice
'Hail' the opportunist!

THE RUMOUR INDUSTRY

They're the ordinary folks
some work some don't
but find time to sit
together and manufacture
rumours at the mill
package them for export
when shipped out
they raise their nostrils
sniffing around for recipes
and materials for the next
batch of rumours
with finesse, these folks
doctor true accounts
of situations
the mountain of their exaggerations
peeks into the heavens
in their gossip industry
and rumour mill
lie sits on a throne
and reigns supreme

MY LITTLE GIRL

My little girl
Comes up to me
Looks me in the eyes
And with her usual smile
Says, 'Daddy can't grow'
My smile greets hers
I think about children's
Innocence and reasoning
My fifteen your old daughter
Remarks, 'Baby, Daddy can't
Grow because he's old
You don't know that?'
I chastise my teen girl
How time flies
It's just the other day
She, a baby, asked me
Childish questions
It's amazing how some
Memories of childhood
Experiences easily slip
Away from people

PREDATOR'S CRY

Bellasha was a fat woman
Who contended over everything
Cursing, swearing and shouting
Were her life
An argument arose
And she pounced on Della,
Her nwunyedi
Floored her and sat on her
Whilst atop Della
Bellasha punched
And thumped, screaming,
'Ogbulanumo!'*
It's strange to hear
The predator howling
That a powerless prey
Is hurting it, the former

'Ogbulanumo' means 'he/she has killed me'

BREXIT

In modern times
many countries of the world
are ensconced in seats
of dependency, and cloaked
in their so-called
globalisation
economic integration
they wait and wait
for financial hand-out
from China and other
super-power
the result: whenever
there's a problem in the super-power
the beggarly, waiting – for – alms
third world begins
to worry and fret
no wonder BREXIT
breeds worries in some nations

CUBA

Ostracised and abandoned
for many, many years
by comity of nations
she refused to reject herself
never despaired
never threw her hands in the air
awaiting death
but her leadership
and her people organised
the society, engaged
in industry and productivity
excellent educational system
and skills training
many years since
the imposition of economic
sanction and blockade, this ship
this Cuba remains afloat
strong and well.

WHY HE LOOKS OUTSIDE

She's no time for her husband
simply occupied and possessed
with occupational undertakings
preoccupied with jostlings
and wranglings
for work place hierarchical elevations
no time to prepare meals
no time to pamper the man
with whom she'd made vows
no time to perform wifely conjugal duties
to the man
She's a stranger
and a foreigner
to her man and to her marriage
unconsciously invited stress
into the marriage
invited centrifugal elements
in the relationship
resulting in loss of companionship
the elements strengthened
the husband turned
determined to look outside
and to work outside
receiving tremendous gratification
not mindful of communal discussion

CYNICS

Some people have nothing
positive and constructive
to offer concerning others
their cynicism and fastidiousness
becloud their minds
so greatly that they can
only see foibles, pitfalls
and 'no-good' in other lives
for this, they belittle others
they are unappreciative of others
they tarnish and sully
the image of others
cynics are a bane
to human development

FITNESS INDEED

He is a driver
a taxi driver
he brags of his links
his connections with some officer
at Vehicle Fitness Centre
this driver gives the officer
some money for assessment
of a vehicle that's parked
miles and miles away
from the centre
the officer certifies the vehicle
fit in absentia
the driver boasts that corruption
is good for the country
as it saves time
to him, without corruption
the system would be painfully
and perpetually slow
But, when the same not-road tested
vehicle certified fit wobbles
skids and kills a pedestrian
relative of the said corruption-loving
driver
then, corruption becomes a bad matter.

AT THE IMMIGRATION DESK

Many years ago I arrived
in this land
the immigration official
to whom I went
refused to grant me entry
instead he called,
through the intercom, his
superior who asked him
to send me to him
from his counter he ordered me
to go to a particular door
not far away
I made a step or two
Then saw the door open
Two hefty officers emerged
And waited for me
I was asked in
Interrogation, questioning and quizzing
Ensued
They said they would not grant me
Entry because of the offences
my countrymen had committed
in their land
whilst decrying those criminal acts
I told them, with respect, that
they were meting out injustice
to me by stereotyping me

I stood my ground as I
expressed that in their own land
there were the good and the bad
and it would be unfairness
of the highest order to punish
me for the sins of others
I asked to be given
a chance to, as an individual,
prove myself or discredit myself
Today, I can say that I have
added great value to this country

The lesson: xenophobia, racism, prejudice,
stereotyping and discrimination
would be no more if people engaged in
appreciation of the uniqueness of individuals

YARDIE STYLE

A stout Japanese young man
emerged from a shop
in the street
he went across to his pal
a Jamaican barber
sitting in front of his barbering
salon
They fist bumped and began
a conversation
this Japanese lit a wrapped
piece he had in hand
pushed it in his mouth
took a draw and let out
a cloud of smoke
My friend standing beside me
across the street said, 'Hmm,
look at him behaving as if
he's used to marijuana'
His eyes quickly turned red
We watched him for a while
Life is a cross-cultural
Journey, sometimes.

FRIGHT

Sitting at her desk
that afternoon somewhat
tired because of the heat
in the library
two male students struggled
wrestled, pushed and pulled
at each other
outside
on the corridor
One bent low and taking up
a machete chased the other
into the library
impelled by great fright
she sprang up and dashed off
leaving her high-heeled shoes behind
totally forgetting about us
who were using the library
facilities at the time

TYRANTS' LIVES

They are afraid
of something, some negative
situations
so they mask their fear
with arrogance and high – handedness
to their subjects they talk tough
and flaunt their coated fearlessness
but beneath this façade
lie deep-seated cowardice
insecurity, weakness and inadequacy
it's sad that they use
the apparatus of the state
to perform their acts of ruthlessness
trampling of human rights
they employ every means
to hold tenaciously to power
they 'work' indefatigably to perpetuate
their regime not minding
they, themselves, are human
and that humans are creatures of time and
dust.

HURTFUL SOUND

Christmas Eve evening
I was going through a street
downtown when I saw
a teenaged mother cuddling
a four day old baby
beside two mountains of sound
boxes blaring out unholy music
the intensity of the sound made
my adult heart twitch

As she rocked to the music
my soul was awash with
pity for the hurt being done
to the innocent baby's heart
the musician was asking in the song
'Want a proper fix, call me?'
I shook my head, and muttered
That the irresponsible mother
Needed a proper fix in her head.

REMEMBERING MY FAMILY

I grew up in a family
so close and closely -
knit, ever ready
to help one another with passion
with strong feeling
of love and affection
coursing through our being
we lived together during affliction
and in times of rejoicing
when I engage in reflection
of my childhood living
there is a saturation
of my being
with nostalgic feeling

A SHREW

The thoughtlessness that suffuses
her mind and her being never amuses
me
how an educated woman
behaves unintelligently
issues arise, her approach
is to use fight
and aggression as solutions
when one tries to show
her the error of her ways
one is insulted, shouted at
and cursed
her approach
is indeed a reproach

WHEN THEY CAME

White missionaries came
to the village
they came with their creed
which they passed on to the people
some villagers received it
as a life-changing message
male converts from *Okwaraebezie*
family were touched
deeply touched
and seriously touched
hitherto they were polygynous
but because of their new faith
they sent away bevies of wives
only leaving 'their first loves'
whom they shortly took
to the altar
their passion for their new faith
had consumed them
but grief now reigned
in the hearts of their ex-wives
What a personification
of the joy and pain of proselytization!

BENA

Bena was issued a visa
for domestic job oversees
she danced and shouted for joy
and made some unkind remarks
as though we were against
her progress
we let things be, however
years passed, many years passed
we learnt that Bena had been
in a state shelter
based on some trumped up
allegations she had made
against her employers
now living everyday life
we wonder if she
wouldn't have been better off
with the thriving agro business
she had, before she left home
it would seem the grass
isn't so green on the other side.

THE BROKEN CALABASH

They made a plan to go
to that community
a seven hour journey
the day before, the *udu**
which was to be taken
there smashed
one elder told them to
not go on the journey
to refrain from the marriage
rites
but they rejected his advice
after the rites had been performed
they began to head home
that was when it happened
thirteen persons lost their lives
a tragedy which shook the clan
a river of tears flowed
but spilled oil could not be recovered

**udu* – an African gourd or calabash used to store water or palm-wine

THE BOMB

I came home from school
and heard that a bomb
had been discovered
by the builders
 who were digging
the foundation for a relative's house
it was a missile
from the Biafra – Nigeria war
some ten years before
the labourer whose spade
had struck it was riddled
with goose-bumps
and ripples of fright
down his spine
how he could've been blown
in pieces but for God's mercy
the authorities were informed
my family was asked to evacuate
the compound early that morning
the experts detonated the bomb
there was deafening plosive sound
the elements were flung
and scattered miles away
I was at school
wondering if everything was alright
at home
I wouldn't know until

I reached home
I wouldn't kwon. Wouldn't know
yet I kept wondering
what an agony!

BLURRED CONTEMPLATION

She's beginning to feel
The first stirrings of love
so nothing else matters
to her ……………. Now
she is dazed
stunned and consumed
by this intense feeling
is it really love
or infatuation?

As it is if death
stares her in the face
she's not going to be moved
just because of her feelings
just because of love
but, does he really mean it?
his words, his overtures
and his moves have tattered
her to this spot
yet he is as free as a bird.

THE DELUSIONAL LEADER

He was assigned this plant
many years ago
before his arrival
the plant was not bad
Now, with his bipolar personality
he runs the enterprise
his system, his way
of handling the affairs of the plant
is epileptic and schizophrenic
the empire is dying
under his watch
yet he thinks he is the best
thing that life has been blessed
with
he creates ruins
and calls them milestones
and achievements
he is a producer of toxin
in the ergonomics of the institution.

MISDEEDS AND REGRETS

She joins the group
called 'the Outlaw'
skips classes
hanging out with the boys
gradually and imperceptibly
killing her future
it's a great joy
for her to disrespect teachers
and adults in the community
a pleasure sowing evil seeds
if only she knew what's lurking
the future awaiting her

But, naturally we're blind
nay short sighted
until reality dawns on us
the harvest of the bad seeds
planted years back
is reaped – a harvest
of sorrow, pain and regret
the present reverberating
with 'Had I known'
trying to 'right' those ancient
wrongs becomes an uphill task
So, youth watch yourself.

DANGER IS THRILLING

'Danger is thrilling'
Emilin told me
I, initially, was taken
aback by her statement
then, I recovered
and found that statement
deep and profound
'Could this be the reason
humans pay no heed
to warnings, go ahead
and court trouble?'
I asked myself
I see the truth
in Emilin's statement
in good, educated and
decent women going
after terrible, irresponsible
and criminal-minded men
and settling with them
in relationships
I see the truth
in Emilin's statement
in the majority electing
a dangerous, inhumane and soulless
candidate into a public office!

CAMILLE

Her name is Camille
she's made my life a corn-meal
of real, real, real
trouble like one employed to stingy Oneal
she causes me pain
like there's a nail
in my vein
she's put my life in jail
Camille, Camille
you're the dangerous real
deal

'SHEINSPIRATION'

She is an inspiration
to me in times of tribulation
for sometimes I've an inclination
to cause a cessation
of good occupation
because of social vilification
which engenders provocation
but she engages in promotion
of my artistic contribution
to the development of this generation
so when the temptation
arises for termination
of my artistic production
I hold on to her message of determination

THE VOTERS

I heard the voice of democracy say
"I am the way
To go and people should follow me"
so I see
people deceive incumbents
aspirants
and pollsters
swelling up crowds
at election campaigns
fecundating the mass of supporters
election day arrives
the people turn and vote
for their last minute choiced candidate
making the other candidate
weep, grieve and mourn
causing pollsters to frown

WHITE SEPULCHURE

This place is festooned
with eye catching elements,
beautiful to the brim
but, beneath this façade
lie rot, ruin and rust
it's an institution of ill repute
entrenched mediocrity
unchecked indiscipline
unbridled animosity and hostility
barefaced nepotism and favouritism
perpetrated by the Head
a head who hypocritically
talks about 'fairness' and 'equity'
but doesn't exemplify such virtue.

FATHER CHRISTMAS

My maternal uncle took my sister
and me to Father Christmas
I was four then and my sister two
Father Christmas (Santa Claus)
beckoned us but I refused
to go to him
'cause his white beard
and looks were so surreal
that my innocent mind was gripped
by fear
he showed us beautiful toys
and gifts but I never budged
my uncle made to take me
to him but I screamed
almost creating
a scene
my sister, however, went
to Father Christmas, shook
hands with him
and had a chat with him
I stood at a distance
watching them
afterwards, Father Christmas gave
her gifts, and told her that some
of the gifts were for me
while we were leaving
I was looking at him

with misgiving and deep
sense of awe

THE NEW DRIVER

The new driver sitting
stiffly behind the wheel
beads of sweat coursing
down her face
stops at the stop-light
a few minutes evaporate
RED changes to GREEN
It's time to drive
through the dreaded flat-bridge
she fidgets, freezes and becomes frigid
a cacophony of tooting vehicle horns
from behind and before the narrow bridge
she lunges the car forward
heading for the waters
swiftly a passenger beside her
grips the steering, wheeling it
away from tragedy
the driver slams the brake
halting the car in the middle
of the bridge
interminable lines of traffic
form
tempers rise, and expletives
and cursing pervade the atmosphere

THE PASTOR AND THE MAD WOMAN

Pastor, an ecclesiastical big shot,
was cruising through a ghetto like
community
a woman stark naked
one at the car
smashing the back windscreen
on the right
the suddenness of the episode
and the sound shook and shocked
him
he couldn't stop immediately
there was long line of traffic behind
after a yard he parked
his car and quickly alighted
to survey the damage
he took a few steps to see
the culprit but the lunatic
gave out a loud shout
grimaced and began to dance
dancing to some unheard music
dancing to unsung song
known only to her
her naked body completely
powdered with dust and dirt
a picture of delirium
confused

the Minister of Religion went
back into his car
he was slated to be
at a church
convention
but now seething with anger
being eaten on the inside
with rage he drove to a police station
to make a report of the incident
he arrived late at the holy convocation
whilst the praise and worship session
was going on
he was outside making phone calls
overseas
nothing, nobody called cheer him up
he left the convocation
before the pronouncement of benediction

FIRST CLINICAL EXPERIENCE

The young men and women
dressed neatly in their white laboratory coats
looking resplendent and royal
their gaits expressing grace
and terrestrial majesty
they told the rest of us
in the citadel of learning
the ivory tower
that they were more important than we were
they were the future doctors, pathologists,
anatomists and oncologists
that they were the medical pharmacologists
and medical laboratory scientists
of tomorrow
they bragged and bragged about
one morning they got on
the university bus, exuding splendour
destination: the University Teaching
Hospital
it was the start of their clinical programme
reaching,
they were ushered into a large room
door securely locked now
by a professor of Anatomy
he pressed three buttons
and a hundred drawers
flew open with cadavers

the under graduates were frightened
'Students, take the instruments
on the tables, and vertically dissect
the cadavers (dead bodies)' said
the professor
instantly, many students rushed
to the door, opting to go
back to their hostels
but, the door was securely locked
no escape, no escape!
Evening came,
They returned to the campus
Looking dejected, eyes red
Some dumbstruck
Some dashed into beer parlours
To calm their nerves down with alcohol
We, the non-medical students
Had a good laugh
Nevertheless, we consoled them
And encouraged them
Never to give up on their dreams
LIFE GOES ON

I have felt
the anguish that comes
from failure
I know the pain
of debacle
I know for real

I have tasted
the joys of success
I have savoured
the sweetness of victory
and basked in euphoria
that life offers sometimes
I truly have, I truly have

One thing I do know
is that life
has her vicissitudes
so, success or failure
life has to go on
but, I will keep trying
I will fight the good fight

PHONE CALL ON THE BUS

On a bus in London
one evening she takes
out her cellular phone
and calls her workplace
'My grandmother is going
to die tonight. That's
what the doctor said.
If she dies tonight,
I'm not working tomorrow'
she said in her crisp
British accent
an eerie feeling saturates
my brother's psyche
because in our world
and culture death is not
a phenomenon that's spoke of
cavalierly, casually and glibly
instead it's considered an enemy
that shouldn't form the object
of a discourse except when it strikes

GRIEF and DILEMMA

She prepared herself
physically for the thanksgiving
service of her departed dear seed
shortly after his demise
she began to wear her wedding
ring which she had put aside
for many, many moons
her estranged husband
understandably would fly
in from the Big Apple
for the occasion
at the wake the man
she had been flirting with appeared
initially, she froze
afterwards regained her composure
and resolved to ignore him
she kept her paramour
at arm's length
but he slighted
and began to act up
her emotion now a potpourri
of dilemma and grief
she broke down
but her release from
this custody of agony
came when her best friend's
husband, a police officer, took

away that pest of a man
for boisterous behaviour

IT SHALL BE WELL

As I face the challenges
struggles, failures and disappointments
of this life
I say to myself
'It shall be well with me'

As I feel the emotional pains
choreographed by the strife
conflicts, adversities and toils
of this life, I say to myself
'It shall be well with me'

Fighting against the current
of the waters
it's so strong I'm tossed
but I choose to stay
the course in this journey

I know it'll be well with me
I feel it'll be well with me
I believe it'll be well with me
I declare that it'll be well with me
I shout 'It'll be well with me!'

My words echo across the ocean
My words resonate with optimistic humanity
My words soar into the heavenly

Barriers must be broken
'cause it must be well with me.

ATTEMPTED RAPE

The boys were in class
waiting for the instructor
who was not available
the wait seemed so long
there was a lone girl
in their midst
an evil thought arose
in one of the boys
he, like Judas, went
behind her and tightly
held her hands backwards
instigating his peers
to sexually molest her
but she struggled and struggled
shook and shook until
she wrestled free
now free
she scampered off
to report
the incident
to a teacher on a different
block
the boys were punished
for attempted rape
in addition to sexual molestation
charge

JENNY'S SAD STORY

Jenny,
a man in his early forties,
in those days, used to pass by
on his bicycle
on his womanizing missions in the village
one new year's eve
many moons ago,
four of us sat with him
as he outlined his plans
for the soon-to-be new year
I'll be in Europe in the New Year
and as soon as I get there
I'll start womanizing.
For that's my life' he said
Two years later
I heard that Jenny
was killed in Europe
because he was in
a romantic relationship with a married woman
What a sad story!

MANDELA, A HERO

You were truly
a hero
and an icon
for your anti-apartheid stance
for your unwavering belief
in racial equality

You were a hero
for promoting reconciliation
peace and forgiveness
in South Africa
for being a beacon
of such virtue to the world

You were a hero
because you exemplified,
epitomised and personified
respect for the rule of law
democracy and good governance

You my hero
the greatest leader
Africa has ever known
whatever your state
you, Mandela will always stand
tall in my heart and the hearts of many

RIGHT LEADERSHIP'

Seek not leadership
for personal reasons
and self-aggrandizement
but to improve the lives of others

Seek not leadership
as a vehicle for oppressing
others but as a means
of empowering and uplifting humanity

Seek not positions of leadership
as badges of honour
but as opportunities
to work and serve community

Seek not leadership
as an avenue to engage
in skulduggery and corruption
but to promote honesty and moral
uprightness

THE EVICTION ORDER

Here is a nonagenarian
my former landlady
she tells me that she's
been asked to rent
a room outside
that she's to vacate
the house she's been living
in for many years
a house she purchased,
her own property
now, this sixty year old woman
abroad has forgotten the hand
that took care of her
while a child
the one that fended for her
one that sent her to school
she wants to eject
that hand that fed her
this is cruelty of the most
vicious kind and injustice
of the highest order

UNCERTAINTY

We came here
the bastion of democracy
the home of the freedom
but,
we beheld horror
agony, anguish and fear
occasional by the executive order
to remove unauthorised migrants
we who came to find solace
were gripped by despair
anxiety and distress
so,
we decided to move
up north in freezing temperatures
through woodlands blanketed by snow
we travelled by night
a tiring journey
a two year old
worn out and fatigued
by the long journey
stopped, asking to be left
to die rather than tread
this is our state:
rejected by the country we're
leaving behind
uncertain of the treatment
we'll receive across the border

this is our station
this is our condition!

LOST HAIR

At twenty five
when I arrived
in this land
I was full-haired
I went to the barber
got a haircut
rubbing my head during a bath
I had a funny feeling
from that day
my hair line gradually
receded
until I became who I hated
to be as a youth
for I became who I hated
to be as a youth
for I never liked
baldness
this is my agony
this is my broken heartedness
I want my hair back
really want it back
it bothers me much
'cause males don't
wear wig!

THE CUSS FROM ABOARD

He calls his daughter
from the home of the free
she answers. 'Yes, Daddy'
he asks, 'What are you doing?'
'Daddy. I'm eating'
'What type of food are you eating?'
'Yam and ackee, Daddy'

He begins to cuss
and fuss
'I want to come back home
I'm tired of this hell of a place
I'm here feeding on junk food
I miss my home
My home has good, good
food

DESTRUCTION BY NIGHT

I was ironing clothes
at the penultimate hour
to the birth of a new day
when I heard some crashing
sound outside
investigation: one stall outside
hade been pulled down
the culprit: faceless
and nameless
the new day was ten minutes old
still ironing, I heard
the sound of machete chopping
down some wood
I looked through the window
and saw a young woman
looking out
watching out
while her male companion
busily chopped away
at the planks
in no time three stalls
were flattened
shortly, the duo hastened
off
morning fully appeared:
the vendors cussed
fussed

and cursed
suspicion became a wildfire
tempers rose to fever heights
even as they worked
to put pieces together
no sale was made
'cause they had to labour
whole day to restore
their facilities
to operational capacities.

WHEN WILL THEY SEE THEMSELVES?

Mental illnesses beset
some individuals
psycho-social problems grip
some persons
others, normal, are at the mercy
of those with such conditions
but the puzzling issue
is that those with maladies
don't see themselves
as being ill
the healthy are in trouble
the sick, here, are in denial
how can the situation be
reconciled?
when will they see themselves?
it's an irony of life
that those outside looking in
can and do see
but those inside can't see
what is on the inside
so, when will they see themselves?

MURDER OF THE INNOCENT

Ogologo was carrying news
getting people into conflicts
in a ghetto community
one morning
early, early, the time
that sleep is sweetest
some masked men kicked
down the front door
of his dwelling, went in
but didn't see him
his oldest son was there
the men asked him about his father
and he told them he was not around
they pumped several bullets in him
Ogologo was out partying
in another community
when he received the bad news
he moved out of the area
to this day his younger son
holds a serious grouse against him
laying his brother's death
at his father's feet.

STRESS AND YOU

Stress puts lives to the test
and robs people of their rest

Stress shows many signs
behavioural, emotional and physical signs

Stress does not play
but causes death and decay

So, stress should not be toyed
with, but be destroyed

To deal with it
you must ear right

To get rid of it
you should exercise and be fit

To eliminate stress
you should take time to rest

To kill stress
you should associate with optimists

WHAT A SHEPHERD

He ties the goats
near the house where I live
a roll of marijuana
sticking out of his mouth
the poor creatures stay
in the open for a week or more
before he remembers them
some of them
on the verge of death
during parturition
some,
near strangulation by the tether
save for the timely intervention
of a good Samaritan
from my household
this callous goat-herder
leaves me saying
'What a shepherd.'

TO SERVE AND PROTECT

The land has become a hot-bed
of crime and violence
even as the police promise
to serve and protect the people
sometimes, however, when crime
or violence is taking place
and one calls the station
the police deliberately take
unconscionably long time
to come out of the station
to crawl out of the shell
by then the deed is already done
what a way to serve and to protect
the people of the land!

CAPTURED BY A REJECT

In my youth I respected
teachers but despised
their profession
saw them as people in an occupation
earning pitiable
miserable
and pathetically meagre remuneration
after university graduation,
I was offered a teaching position
but flatly rejected it
was afraid it
would pauperize me
now in a foreign land, it
hit me
that the career so despised
captured
me
arrested
me,
and holds me.

MUMMY'S PHONE

She sticks her tiny index finger
presses some buttons on the phone
numbers, letters, hashtag
and other signs
puts the phone on her right ear
'Hello Uncle'
Hello Aunty'
shouts, 'Mummy nobody is answering
my call'
flings the phone on the bed
getting into a very hot tantrum
kicking the air with her small feet
crying, screaming and yelling
fill the room

INSTITUTION OF MARRIAGE

'Marriage is an institution'
people, sometimes, mention
but, I make an indication
that in it, when wrong, I'll take correction
without allowing institutionalization
of self, will not accept imposition
of life regimentation
never let me be imprisoned by marriage's regulation
nevertheless, I recognise its contribution
to the health of home and nation

I'LL TRY NO MORE

How can you say
you love me
yet, you mistrust
and distrust me?
I bare my heart before you
still, you have no confidence
in my words
and in my intentions
I guess this is the reason
some live hidden
secretive and 'sealed' lives
while relationships
after donkey years,
I now realise I can't
convince you to trust me
even after crossing several oceans
and climbing formidable mountains
to prove my trustworthiness
I've truly worked indefatigably
so as to earn your trust
but you deliberately denied me
what would've been my earnings
so, from this moment I'll try
no more
take it however you will
I'll try no more

THE SUN WILL SHINE ON ME

The sun will shine on me
though the clouds are heavy
dark and angry

The sun will shine on me
though the winter of life
belches and spews out frost and ice

The sun will shine on me
though the downpour has drenched
and soaked me like a bird bedraggled

I see these conditions
I face these situations
But, I know, the sun will shine on me again

The sun will shine on me again
She will shine again
and I will feel her warmth again

She will shine on me
So, I stay strong
and wait, no matter how long!

GIVE ME BACK THOSE DAYS

The way nowadays is not the way
it used to be
not the communal effort
of raising the child
being our neighbours' keeper
the fellow feeling in the heart
has evaporated from the present reality
man has no soul anymore
and is now as cold as technologies
and robots
so, I ask for the past
give me back those days
of togetherness
those days of true self
those days without plastic smiles
those days when hearts
were not masked
but were felt and true
give me back those days
when humans communed
and dialogued with Mother Nature.

THE SEVERED CORD

He stood by the graveside
reading the eulogy
he had crafted on the life
of his beloved sister
in a voice so tremulous
he severed it, severed that cord
that bound us together
we thought, afterwards, it was
a product of emotional overflow
but, he meant it
he meant it
our mother's siblings meant it
times and times and times again
we tried to reach out to them
but they rebuffed us
so we schooled ourselves
to accept their coldness
towards us
we steeled ourselves against
their coldness
towards us
we mourn the death of our mother
but we don't bemoan the severed cord.

THE DRIVER

The driver stops by the roadside
near a pub
he saunters in for some
alcoholic drinks
after awhile, he staggers out
and fondles his left pocket
he takes out his car key
turns it, stomps the pedal
the metallic structure roars
lunges, flies across the road
lands on a pole near a stone wall
the vertical structure cuts in two
its top suspended by cable lines
by this time, the pub spews out
alcoholics, gamblers and strip-dancers
the man slouched on the wheel
is he gone into eternity or
is he in an alcoholic – engendered
stupor?

SIGNATURE OF CHARM

The sun was full
though the evening was setting in
as the gentle breeze
blew over the sea
I took in the beauty of nature
the panoramic view
of the expanse of water
and the white sandy beach
filled my heart with glee
this is Negril, Jamaica
Nature's signature of charm and beauty
God's masterpiece of the splendour
of creation

SUN AND THE RAIN

The rain came down
accompanied by the wind
but, the sun appeared
giving a smile
her smile belied
the heaviness of the heavens
So, I wondered if it would be
a ding-dong affair
I wondered if the smile
of the sun, though under threat,
would prevail
to lighten the day
I wondered if the heaviness
of the clouds would unleash
torrential rain
but, the rains came down
in slants
feigning seriousness initially
suddenly, the sun burst
the clouds again and held
on for sometime
I was awe-struck that the earth
could be blessed by both
natural elements.

ADDICTION DIED

My daughter was addicted to the internet
or as she called it "The net"
This attachment to "The net"
Made me fret

Her misery, her misery
occasioned by non-reception of internet
signal
most times evoked my fury
until we reached the final

The final, the final
Came when some criminal
Cut the phone line
Into elements so fine

So, my daughter returned to the past
when she used to read
she got back to her books – fast
to meet her need

Her misery
And my fury
Vanished
Because the addiction had died.

EVERYDAY

Every day I sit
at the foot
of the great teacher
called LIFE
and I learn

Every day I see
the never-ending story
called LIFE
unfold
new experiences I behold

Every day I look
at the mountains of challenges
and problems called LIFE
but somewhere in – between lie possibilities
which I observe

Every day, LIFE
Dishes out things to us
Pleasant and unpleasant
Bitter-sweet sometimes
That's the reality of human existence

PAY DAY

His loose goats
ate his neighbour's vegetables
left the farm in a deplorable state
the neighbour complained
but his heart was impervious
to the plaintive voice of the neighbour
instead, he threatened her
and dismissed her
to him, hers was no plight

Two day later,
thieves came in on him
tied him up and took away
his luxury belongings,
leaving his apartment bare
bereft of leisure
and pleasure-providing gadgets
when the criminals left
he cried out, "Life's not fair!"

SESA 2020

They made frantic
but determined efforts
to pull down
the seventy plus year old colossus

The last three weeks
saw them –
people of powerful interest
tug, push and pull at this political institution

The day came
restlessness became
the temperature of the game
the colossus only being held by a thirty-two
inch steel

Bent but not demolished
disappointed, the powerful interests
retired to their homes
would they try again in four years' time?

Would the colossus be salvaged
(before the next poll) with
Rehabilitation and reconstruction,
Fortification and solidification?

AWESOME ANTS

I watch the ants,
very small creatures
perform
mighty acts
awesome, awesome tasks

I admire their organization
and disciplined way of operation
moving in lines
moving foods

I'm awed by their industry
and their 'thirty' mentality
packing up foods for rainy
days for their family

Ants' unity
creativity
and their productivity
are a great lesson for humanity

THE AGONY OF AN EX-TYRANT

He leads the plant for years
with terror and high-handedness
dehumanizing workers
denying them of their rights
causing cries
and tears
causing groaning

However, he has lackeys
sycophants and tale-bearers
whom he grooms
and places in leadership positions
to these he dishes out insults
at meetings
in public gatherings

The stooges take his insults
with hypocritical smiles
they embrace all his wiles
and machinations
with plastic grins

Like all life's events
his tenure expires
he mandatorily retires
and from the office he exits

Now, the ex-stooges
his former sycophants
sever links, with him and cut ties
and against him build fences

So, the former boss
is steeped in restlessness
and emotional stress
for the loss of the power to oppress

BEFORE AND AFTER

They feel that their biological clock
is ticking
and time is going

They yearn for rings
to be put on their fingers
signalling security in relations

At this point they pamper
and dote on their men
going to extremes for them

After the nuptials
the pomp and pageantry
life takes a different turn

No more spoiling
of men, no more pampering
no more doting

"You're mine now
I can do as I like
You're no longer sought after"

Yet, when the men seek attention
and affection
elsewhere, there's tension

NOT BROKEN

I was imprisoned by life's circumstances
fettered by human evil machinations
shackled by the treacherous acts
of people I trusted
it seemed as though the dungeon
had become my eternal abode
in the face of this strong inhibition
I made a decision to free
my inner being
Yes, the powers and authorities could jail
the outer me
belonged to me
I could set my inner me free
so I chose to smile within
I chose to dance on the inside
I chose to celebrate my worth
even though I was subjected to indignity
I elected to cherish my human dignity
the external was in pain, agony and turmoil
but through a deliberate and conscious effort
the internal was not only free
but in bliss
no one could do that for me
but me
no one could divorce the external
and the internal
but me

no one could partition between the outer
and the inner
but me
I chose to be the caption of my inner vessel
as the oppressive forces
bound the outer me
Yes, when they thought they had won
I had victory on the inside
So, they could not destroy me
because of my indescribably great inner
strength
I withstood the heinous acts,
ill-treatment meted out
by my adversaries
I turned their well-crafted 'darkness'
over my life
into my bright and sunny day
Yes, yes, I did not just survive
I overcame
I grew stronger
I became steelier to the gusts
and waves of life's adversities
Yes, I was not broken.

GONE TO THE DOGS

I was waiting for the meal
to arrive from the kitchen
did not know when sleep
came and took me away
I must have been in dream land
for roughly an hour
I awoke, looked around
in the living room
hunger and tiredness still
had their heavy arms on me
shortly, I mustered up some strength
to go looking for Uncle George
who was preparing the meal
by the time I dozed off
met him emerging from the outside kitchen
with a tray invaded by plates of food,
vegetables and drinks
his dogs jumping on him
trying to shoo them away
and trying to close the zinced door
the tray tilted
he made to balance it
in the face of the prancing dogs
but,
the edibles all fell
on the sandy ground outside
that was all

nothing was left in the pot
nothing on the tray
my hope was dashed
it went with the foods
the dogs gleefully feasted on the foods
Uncle George let out a shout
of anguish
I left with a stomach gnawed
by hunger

HER MAN

She was just all over the young man
beaming with great joy
especially whenever he stopped by
in his car
in her euphoria she would not
acknowledge the presence of someone
like me
to her I didn't matter
however, when she did speak
to me
she bragged about spending weekends
and extra 'lock down' days
at his place
her jollity continued for sometime
but, one afternoon I saw her
emerging from his room
looking sad and dishevelled
he came out and began
to talk to her
but she was just snarling
and snapping
her visage was very suggestive
of some unpleasant situation
prior to my arrival on the scene
I moved on, never saw her
for three months
the next time I saw her

she was heavily pregnant
she felt uncomfortable in my presence
so, she turned and ambled away
the young man had stopped coming by
to pick her up
she no longer went to spend weekends or
'special days' with him

RAINY VOYAGE

Heavy rain attacked the land
with viciousness
bombarded the land
with furiousness
hunger began to caress
me with terrible hand
feeling helpless
and hopeless,
I made myself a special brand
of dress
with black plastic bag, a touch of finesse
stepped into the rain with braveness
mid way into my rainy voyage
thunder roared
my umbrella suddenly sagged
I, nevertheless, summoned courage
and moved on, walked
was drenched
and bed-draggled
by the time I reached
my cottage

FROM SCHOOL

I was on the street
cooling out
looking out
when I heard
and sighted
our young people returning from school
they were not cool
their conduct was negative
and their speech full of expletive
some were blaring out indecent lyrics
others promoting whoredom
some engaged in different gimmicks
what an evil kingdom
many of our adults are building
and creating
in our youth
in our youth!

MOTHER JA SPEAKS TO HER CHILDREN

I speak to you all, my children
to stop aping the ways
of other lands
I'm your Mother JA
the Gem of the Caribbean
the Queen of the West Indies
your sweet, sweet Jamaica

My scintillating natural beauty
my enthralling dances
my delectable, mouth-watering dishes
my celebrated athletic prowess
my indomitable spirit in adversity
my robust democratic political system
define me as classy and unique

My children, why follow the ways of North America?
As you speak with fake foreign accents
other nationalities love my voice,
my tongue
my sons and my daughters
come back to your real selves
heed the voice of your incomparable Mother JA!

HOW I SEE LIFE

This is how I see life now
a situation in which people
live for themselves
brother no longer knows
his brother
sister no longer cares
about her sister
friends are treachery
waiting to happen
so- called 'lover' is a traitor
behind a mask
this is how I see the world now
a place where people shake
your hand with one hand
and stab you with the other hand
where smiles are not true
but plastic and cosmetic
there is a disconnect between the heart
and the face
where people love you
for what they can gain from you
rather than you being you
where people assess your worth
based on your material possessions
instead of your character
this is how I see life
and the world

THE SYSTEM

There is a system
which is alive
in our human society
A system in which
there is suffering
in the midst of plenty
One in which the have's
continue to have
while the have not's
continue to wallow
in abject poverty
It is a system
in which some have not's
have sunk into squalor
The have's have so much
to feed their pets
while their neighbors
have no morsel
and no grains of food
to eat
Here, the saying 'I love you'
abounds but the poor
and needy are neglected
passed by and despised
Here, the politicians
canvassing for voices
claim to love the poor

Yet when they receive the mandate
they remember not the poor.

THE FATEFUL TREE

The seed germinated
grew into a tree
before the eyes of the people
it grew into a huge
towering tree
tongues wagged
assigning it the supernatural
as it was said to be
the abode of some god and spirits
mortals were afraid to prune it
seeing that as tantamount
to causing deaths of people
for donkey years the tree grew
spread out its branches
over homes and shops in the square
a mini-market rose under it
it sheltered mortals
from the scorching sun
But, during an intense rain one afternoon,
this ancient tree came down
from its roots, killing thirty-one
and injuring sixteen
in retrospect, I say to myself
'Mortals were afraid to fell it
lest the entire village died mysteriously.
Now, the tree took itself out,
yet taking lives.'

Therefore, I ask: 'Are mortals toys in the hands of destiny?'

BELIEF IN DEMOCRACY

I believe that human dignity
should be cherished
in every country
that the rule of law should be respected
in every territory
that human rights should be upheld
in every country and county
that good governance
should be in place
that opportunities for advancement
and human development
should be provided by every government
I believe that democracy
should be mankind's occupancy
even though it is hated
even though it is seriously attacked
by tyrants
by autocrats
by despots
by dictators.

GIVE ME BACK THOSE DAYS

The way nowadays is not the way
it used to be
not the communal effort
of raising the child
being our neighbour's keeper
the fellow feeling in the heart
has evaporated from the present reality
man has no soul anymore
and is now as cold as technologies
and robots
So, I ask for the past
give me back those days
of togetherness
those days of true self
those days without plastic smiles
those days when hearts
were not masked
but were felt and true
give me back those days
when humans communed
and dialogued with Mother Nature.

WINNIE MANDELA

Was courageous and bold to challenge
Injustice, oppression and racism
Never relented in her effort to dismantle
Apartheid
No white supremacist could break her spirit
Imprisonment and isolation couldn't quench
her resolve
Equality and freedom were her goals
(WINNIE)

Mother of the South African nation
Adorable daughter of Madikilezi family
No nonsense woman in quest for black
freedom
Determined to promote African liberation
Energetic and valiant fighter against
inhumanity
Loyal to the cause of liberty
African queen, goodbye! (MANDELA)

THE CHILLY WIND

The chilly wind is here again
It's blowing across the land
with its companion – the rain
it's not the rain
of blessing and blessedness
upon the land
but wickedness
this chilly wind is like a cruel hand
ravaging the land
causing rape and murder
pillage and plunder
nepotism
favouritism
cronyism
it's a chilly wind of corruption
devastation
and deprivation
the chilly wind is here
too cause fear
my dear
it's come again
to cause pain!

THE ROSE PLANT

The plant stands beside the car park
A picture of charm
Its lushness and surrounding greenery
silhouette the cream-colored wall nearby
The stem and limbs are a cornucopia
of prickles
The scintillating pink rose flowers
Entice the eyes that love beauty
But ready to prick the hands
That stretch to pluck them
So. it's a beautiful danger
An object lesson in life
For uncontrolled hands.

HEAVEN'S HEAVINESS

The sun rose early that morning
its radiance seemed to blind
the dwellers of the land
emitting sweltering heat
past midday, dark clouds
intruded, blanketing off the sun
shortly, the heaviness of the heavens
descended upon the land
unleashing torrential rain
the trees became like bedraggled
birds
the gutters, inundated with water,
saw tidal waves of non – degradable
pollutants.

THE SICK GIANT

I championed the cause of the black race
My resources have I spewed into humanity
for their betterment
I sang with unwavering voice the beautiful
song
of peace, love and brotherhood among
nations

In the days of boom
Squandermania and ostentatiousness became
my friends
I named myself "The Giant of Africa"
soon, doom entered my life
I began to be weak

Now, behold 'the Giant'
Lie flat, ailing
Looking pale and emaciated
But, what infirmity pins 'the Giant'
To a sick bed?

He's suffering debilitating headache of
poverty
Cardiological problem of corruption
Malaria of maladministration
Fever of sky-rocketing inflation
Cholera of tribal conflicts

Will the 'Giant' ever rise
from this doldrum of comatose economy
from this thralldom of bad governance
above this conundrum of oil/resource-rich but
poverty-stricken situation?

LETTER FROM PRINCESS JAMAICA

Dear Sons and others
beyond the seas
I write this letter with tears
my heart grieves
and aches
for my sons and daughters
whose lives
are snuffed out by the guns
brought into my shores
by some of you and others
please, consider the tears
cascading the cheeks
of grieving mothers
and relatives
of victims
of your death causing machines
I beg you to ship barrels
of toiletries, goodies and foods
to my shores
without packaging guns
in the barrels
it's time to stop making children fatherless
and women widows
it's time to stop the senseless
blood-letting within my frontiers
I appeal to you, my sons
and others overseas

to make donations
send funds
provide grants
for the welfare of my sons and daughters
living within my shores
rather than ship narcotics and guns
Dear Sons and others overseas
take my advice, save lives!
                      Sincerely yours,
                      Jamaica, The Princess
                      of the West Indies.

MR. DADDY

I did something bad
and my daddy sad
and angry with me

I went to him
started talking to him
but he wouldn't talk to me

I went to Mommy
and told her 'Daddy
angry with me'

Mommy smiled
and said, 'Never mind,
stay with me'

I was not happy
that Daddy
Not talking to me

I left Mommy
and shouted, 'Mr. Daddy,
Mr, Daddy answer me!!'

My daddy,
with a face so smiley
hugged me

I felt very happy.

ABOUT THE AUTHOR

Ugochukwu Durueke is a Nigerian Jamaican writer. He is a recipient of a number of prizes and awards for literature from Jamaica Library Service (JLS) and Jamaica Cultural Development Commission (JCDC). He is also a four time 'Letter of the Day' prize winner, and two time 'Poem of the Week' poet. In 2013, He received a writing fellowship from Art Funk Residency & Initiative in Manchester, United Kingdom.

Mr. Durueke is also the author of the following books: 'AGONY OF NATURE,' 'My Sunrise', 'A MENU OF TROUBLE', 'THE DEADLY DEAL' and 'TESTING YOUR ENGLISH SKILLS'.

www.ingramcontent.com/pod-product-compliance
Lightning Source LLC
Chambersburg PA
CBHW031956080426
42735CB00007B/418